CASTLETON
THROUGH TIME
Dr Liam Clarke

AMBERLEY PUBLISHING

Goosehill Hall
This modern photograph shows the Norman castle overlooking the old Goosehill Hall and its farm buildings. The Peak Cavern Gorge can be seen in the centre of the scene. The tree plantation was planted in the nineteenth century.

First published 2011

Amberley Publishing
The Hill, Stroud
Gloucestershire, GL5 4EP

www.amberley-books.com

Copyright © Dr Liam Clarke, 2011

The right of Dr Liam Clarke to be identified as the Author of this work has been asserted in accordance with the Copyrights, Designs and Patents Act 1988.

ISBN 978 1 4456 0591 3

British Library Cataloguing in Publication Data.
A catalogue record for this book is available from the British Library.

Typeset in 9.5pt on 12pt Celeste.
Typesetting by Amberley Publishing.
Printed in the UK.

Introduction

'Everything connected with Castleton, the repository of romance, an epitome of all the Peak, is interesting'; so said W. Shawcross in 1903. It is still a very romantic village, with many old nooks and corners, tiny windows in houses and little narrow passages leading to ancient folds or yards.

Castleton is situated in the beautiful Hope Valley, about 16 miles from Sheffield. The town is named after the Norman castle built by William Peveril, a son of William the Conqueror. The Castle was later used as a prison for many years. It stands on a hill overlooking the town with ancient access up Goosehill and the Earls Way to the original Norman entrance. The modern entrance is now from the market place.

The Church of St Edmund possibly has Saxon origins but the present building dates from 1100, when it was used as a garrison church for the Castle. Its original name was 'The Church of Peak Castle', changed in the fourteenth century to St Edmund's. There is evidence of a leper house near the village and a hospital, 'The Hospital of St Mary in The Peak', founded by William Peveril's wife. It was in use until at least the mid-1500s. The village also had a number of other buildings used as poorhouses to accommodate the destitute of the village.

In the fifteenth and sixteenth centuries a large number of cottages were built in Castleton without permission, a custom which accounts for many having no land attached to them today. The majority of these homes had just one room downstairs and a space or one room above, and were inhabited by lead miners and weavers. The owners paid rent to the King, and in the late nineteenth century these cottages were allowed to become freehold.

A number of larger houses were built over the years, such as Goosehill Hall, which is still standing and possibly dates back to the fourteenth century. The New Hall, built in the 1470s and demolished in 1890, was situated on the Buxton Road, where the present Methodist church now stands. Possibly one of the earliest domestic buildings in the village is the thirteenth-century Castleton Hall, situated in the Market Place, part of which was also a tithe barn. The building was once owned by Sir Archibald Grant who, because of irregular financial dealings in 1732, was expelled from the House of Commons and spent some time in the notorious Fleet Prison as a bankrupt. He later sold the building to a local solicitor, Micah Hall, in 1754 for £240. It is now a youth hostel.

By the eighteenth century Castleton had become a tourist centre, catering for those travellers who came to see Peak Cavern, the Castle and the parish church. A number of inns, public houses and beer houses were established to meet the needs of these visitors. At one time in the nineteenth century, as many as fifteen hotels or public houses existed to meet these demands. The gift shops remained open seven days a week to satisfy the visitors, a fact which shocked a local visitor, Dr Plumptre.

Today the village is visited by thousands of tourists a year who come to see the four caverns, the Castle, gift shops, tea rooms and the local museum run by the Castleton Historical Society. Lead mining has disappeared and the farming community dwindles each year. Only the gift shops and tea rooms thrive now.

Winnats Pass
This scene is of Winnats Pass in winter, the main road into Castleton from the west in the eighteenth century. Castleton was then just a number of farms with buildings in the centre of the rural village. To travel up or down Winnats Pass then was very dangerous and passengers often had to dismount from the stagecoach or carriage and walk the steep gorge. It is still a very desolate place in winter.

Castleton, 1850s and 1865

This is an early photograph of Castleton viewed from Peveril Castle. The cottages on the west side of the churchyard were still standing in the 1860s but the public right of way which crosses the churchyard form south to north east was removed by an act of parliament in 1861. You can, in the 1850s scene, see the young poplar trees which were planted on the east side in 1802.

Castleton, 1883 and 2011

Houses on the west side of the churchyard have been removed to enlarge the burial ground and new trees have also been planted. To the north-east in this photograph can be seen the recently built Losehill Hall, and to the north of the village the old candle factory. A new large house, The Lodge, has also been built to the east of the church. The village is greener now than in the past.

Losehill Hall, 1922 and 2011

Robert How Ashton, a local landowner, built Losehill Hall, moving from his residence of Cryer House in Castle Street in 1882. The estate was later sold in 1922, after his death. In 1954 it became a Co-operative Youth Centre and it passed to the Peak Park Authority in 1961 to become a study centre. In 1967 the extension illustrated in the 2011 photograph was built to house classrooms.

Losehill Hall Lodge, 1882 and 2011
The lodge to Losehill Hall was built in 1882 and is now a private residence situated on the Castleton–Hope Turnpike Road, built in 1758. This road possibly followed a medieval route way from Hope to Castleton. The main gate to the Hall was moved in the 1960s to allow for the entrance of modern traffic. The lodge itself has not undergone any changes of note since its building in 1882.

Spital Bridge, 1904 and 2011

Spital Bridge is on the site of an ancient river crossing which joined the site of the Hospital of Saint Mary in the Peak, built before 1330, and the village. The existing bridge was built when the turnpike road was established in 1758. This photograph shows the 1st Volunteer Battalion Northumberland Force marching over the bridge to their summer camp in 1904. The bridge was widened in the mid-twentieth century.

Spital Bridge, 1910 and 2011
This later view of Spital Bridge looking west towards the village at the beginning of the twentieth century shows late nineteenth-century housing development. By 2011 this housing development has increased and all electrical cables have been placed underground. In the earlier photograph can be seen the sheep wash used until the late nineteenth or early twentieth century.

The Blacksmith Shop, Spital Bridge, 1917 and 2011
A blacksmith shop was situated on the north corner of Spital Bridge and was housed in a corrugated iron building which had been removed from 'Tintown', Birchinlee. Birchinlee housed the workers building the Howden and Derwent dams, which were completed in 1916. The house in the left of the photograph was also a tin hut, which by 2011 had developed into the building shown in the later photograph.

How Lane, 1909 and 2011

How Lane was not a very busy thoroughfare in 1909. Here we see a lone motorist leaving Castleton along the road to Hope. New housing can be seen on the right. The partially built Methodist church can also be seen through the trees on the left of the picture. This building now serves as the Castleton Village Hall. How Lane today is a very busy thoroughfare.

Derwent House, How Lane, 2011 and 1900
The headmaster of Castleton School from 1885 to 1922 is shown here in 1900 outside his home, Derwent House in How Lane. The house was built in 1895. A hedge has now replaced the iron railings, which were removed to contribute towards the war effort.

Swiss House Restaurant, How Lane, 1950s and 2011
Swiss House Restaurant was built in 1896 as hotel accommodation for passengers who would have used the proposed railway branch line of the Hope and Castleton Light Railway. The railway never materialised and the building has served as a restaurant, bake house and grocer's shop from which bread was delivered by pony and trap in the 1920s. It is now a very comfortable bed and breakfast.

Barnby House, How Lane, 1950s and 2011
Barnby House, on How Lane, is a converted farm barn. In the 1950s the part of the building on the right was a Blue John and jewellery shop. It is now a sweet shop and private residence.

The Cheshire Cheese Public House, How Lane, 1919 and 2011

It is the custom of the Garland Possession to stop outside all the public houses on Garland Day. Here the King, with the flower headdress, and his Consort, played until 1955 by a man, are seen outside the Cheshire Cheese, a seventeenth-century hostelry. In the 1930s the famous male impersonator Vesta Tilley, 'Burlington Bertie', stayed at this pub with her husband, the Conservative MP Lord De Frece.

The Cheshire Cheese Public House, How Lane, 1910 and 1940s
There were at least fifteen public inns or beer houses in Castleton Parish at one time. Only six are left. This scene outside the Cheshire Cheese shows a group of early motorcyclists resting outside the Cheshire Cheese. The Cheshire Cheese started out as a farm, and in the 1940s photograph the stable block can be seen. The door behind the cyclists in the earlier scene has been has been blocked up.

The Peak Hotel, How Lane, 1932 and 2011

The Peak Hotel was the venue for many political gatherings and celebrations such as Queen Victoria's Diamond Jubilee in 1897. A New Year's Ball was held every year in the Pavilion, which was situated opposite the hotel. The old weighing machines outside Barnby House have long been removed, as has the balcony outside the main upper window.

Bus Turnabout, How Lane, 1930s and 2011
In the 1930s the building on the right was a stable in which the Eyre family kept their horses. It was pulled down in 1953 to make way for the bus station. The building to the left, now a bed and breakfast, was a livery stable.

Mill Lane, 1910 and 2011

Mill Lane is an ancient public right of way leading to the 800-year-old, water-driven Corn Mill and medieval Saw Mill. In the early twentieth century the mills were operated by the Eyre family. This scene shows large tree trunks being delivered to the saw mill in 1910. The Corn Mill was housed in the building on the left. The site is now owned by Wearnes Hollingsworth, who manufacture electrical components.

The Barn, Foxhill, 1960 and 2011
This old barn backed onto the leet that served the Corn Mill waterwheel. It was also situated near the old coffin route used by people in Edale village who brought their dead to Castleton for burial before 1634. This ancient right of way continued up to the 1960s – it ran through what is now Rose Cottage Tea Rooms. This old barn and cottage was replaced with a modern building in the 1970s.

Castleton Social Centre and Reading Rooms, Millbridge, 1900s and 2011
This old photograph shows a group of Castleton men outside the Social Centre and Reading Room built by R. Howe Ashton in the late 1800s. Over the years it served as a social centre, school meals kitchen, Parish Council meeting room and doctor's surgery. It is now a private residence.

Eyre's Farm, Millbridge, 1950 and 2011
A very old farm stood on this site until 2008, when the outbuildings were demolished to make way for a modern housing development. The 1950s photograph shows the large farm hay loft before development.

Peper Hall, Milbridge, 1950 and 2011

'Peper Hall' or Pauper Hall – oral tradition would have this building as an old leper house, but it was more likely used for putting up people who arrived at the village gate nearby after curfew and were not allowed into the village until daybreak. The building is mentioned in a set of farmer's accounts in 1791. It was demolished and replaced by private housing.

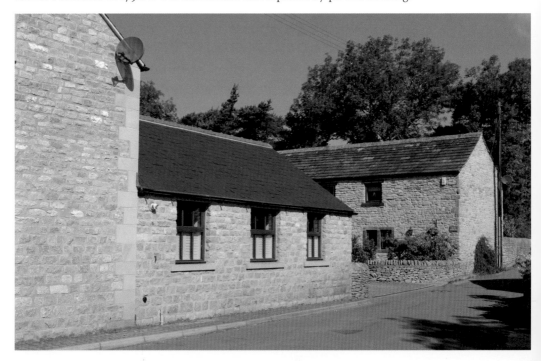

Millbridge Cotton Mill and Weaving Shed, 1970 and 2011

This mill was owned by John and Ellis Eyre in 1819. It was operated as a cotton mill and weaving shed and later used as farm buildings. Castleton has had a number of cotton mills over the years, notably the larger eighteenth-century water-driven cotton mill at Spital Bridge, now a ruin. Weaving was also carried out in individual homes. The Millbridge site is now a private residence.

Trickett Gate House, Millbridge, 1905 and 2011
Trickett Gate House, in the centre of this view, is a fine example of a Derbyshire Long House built before 1455. The part towards the left would have been where the animals were kept and the right-hand section was living accommodation. The building had a stone staircase leading to the sleeping quarters on the first floor. These photographs show the building in 1905 and 2011. It is now three cottages.

The Nag's Head, Cross Street, Late Nineteenth Century and 2011
The Nag's Head was a seventeenth-century inn. The stable block shown on the left was demolished to widen Back Street. Coaches left this hostelry for Hope Station on a regular basis in the early twentieth century.

Castleton School, 2011 and 1890s

This school was erected in 1863 on the site of the old poorhouse. The 2011 scene shows a building, to the right of the school, used as an earlier school, the Armstrong Ladies Boarding School of 1831. The first recorded school master in Castleton is Stephen Hall, in 1687. The 1890s photograph shows Mr Eyre, headmaster, and Miss Barber, a teacher, with village children outside the school.

The Old Bus Station, Back Street, the 1950s and 2011
In the 1850s, omnibuses ran to Sheffield three times a week. On Sundays, the Lucy Long omnibus also ran to Sheffield. Sheffield Corporation ran buses to the village until 1941. Later, Pashley Buses and North Western Buses ran services to Sheffield from Back Street until the new bus station was opened in 1953. Here we see a bus waiting to depart from the old bus station in the early 1950s.

Methodism in Castleton

Castleton had a number of Methodist chapel buildings in the late nineteenth and early twentieth century. The building shown below was the Primitive Methodist Chapel until the building in How Lane, now the village hall, was completed in 1909. The building in the photograph above was a Methodist church, which in the early twentieth century became a 'Pop' or lemonade factory, owned by Mr Boam.

Bray House, The Market Place, 1910 and 2011

In 1910 Bray House was a grocer's shop run by Charles Hopkinson. In the nineteenth century, part of it was a warehouse belonging to a local flax dresser. The front of the building was later demolished to make the entrance road to Pindale wider and safer when motor traffic increased. It is now a private residence.

Bargate Cottage, The Market Place, 1910 and 2011
Here we see Mr Wray outside Bargate Cottage, originally three or four cottages situated near the medieval Bargate. This 'gate' was on the old road to Hope through Pindale. The building was a shop for very many years. It is now bed and breakfast accommodation.

Cave Dale and Bargate, 1900 and 2011

Here we have another view of the Pindale Road, looking west, showing Bargate Cottage to the right of the white-walled cottage in the centre of this scene. The white lime-covered cottage is on the 50-mile-long 'Limestone Way', which includes sections of Saxon trails and Roman roads. It runs through Cave Dale, just above this cottage, through Derbyshire into Staffordshire.

The Pindale Road to Hope and Tideswell, 1930 and 2011
This gentleman is pushing his wheelbarrow along the old road from Pindale. The building in this scene is the Old Needle Factory, now a private residence. The track to this factory ran to the village rubbish dump, and also to the site of a very old farm house, the only farm to be built on the north side of the valley, 'Redseats', the home of the Staley family, which no longer exists.

Black Rabbit Hamlet, Pindale, 1910 and 2011

The brick archway to the left of this scene is the remains of a lime burner's kiln. The shaft that the lime was burned in can be seen above the arch. The last lime burning was carried out by Mr Bramhall, who lived in Black Rabbit and had fifteen sons. All the buildings became derelict during the late nineteenth century. The 2011 photograph show the remains of the old Black Rabbit pub in the trees.

Castleton War Memorial, the Market Place, 1923 and 2011
The war memorial in the market place was dedicated in 1923. This dedication scene illustrates how open the market place was at that time. The large tree planted for Queen Victoria's Jubilee is not as prominent as in 2011. Bray Cottage can be seen in the background before the front part of the building, a shop front in 1910, was demolished to widen the roadway.

Castleton Market Place, 1895 and 2011

Medieval towns were usually built around a market place or church. In 1222 Castleton had as big a market as Derby, with over seventy-one stalls. No large market has been held for hundreds of years on this site. A number of working carriages can be seen outside the barn. This barn is now the outdoor shop and the small lean-to cottage to its left has been demolished.

Castleton Market Place, Early 1903 and 2011

Another view of Castleton Market Place, with Bean Hill Farm barn to the left of the picture. To the right can be seen a four-wheel coach waiting by the Nag's Head Hotel coach house to take travellers to Hope Station. The Norman castle can be seen towering over the village. The War Memorial is now enclosed by railings.

Castleton Market Place, 1920 and 2011

Castleton Market Place was originally twice the size; however, over the years local villagers built cottages that encroached on the market square space as the market declined. Here we see some of these encroachments as cottages and barns on the north side. The wall enclosing the cottages on the left has now been removed and the area in front of the building is today enclosed and registered as common land.

Castleton Hall, the Market Square, 1900 and 2011

Parts of Castleton Hall originate in the thirteenth century. This photograph shows the Hall in 1910 before becoming a Youth Hostel in 1943. The Hall was owned in the eighteenth century by Sir Archibald Grant, who was expelled from Parliament for irregular financial dealings. The door to the north wing, which was used as a manor court, has now been blocked up. The large yew tree now over-shadows the front of the Hall.

The Castleton Garland Ceremony, Market Square, 1911 and 2011

This view shows the finale of the Castleton Garland Ceremony. Local children are Maypole dancing in the Market Square in front of the old Hall. In medieval times the square also served as a bull ring, where the sport of bull baiting took place. To the left of the Hall is a building advertising the services of the nearby Peveril Hotel.

The Peveril Hotel, Market Square, 1905 and 2011

The Castleton Silver Band is seen posing for this photograph outside the Peveril Hotel in 1905. This building had served as the Ship Inn public house since at least 1828, so-called because the roof timbers are reputed to have been made from ships' timbers. The building later became a bank before reverting to a private residence.

Farran House, Castle Street, 1904 and 2011

This old photograph shows Farran House. To the left can just be seen a barn, now demolished. To the left of the barn was the house of Mr Nall, the Parish Clerk in the 1800s, which later became the Ole in't Wall public house, now gone. Farran House, the residence of an eccentric vicar of Castleton from 1780 to 1817, is now a holiday cottage.

Castle Street, 1930s and 2011
Tourism has played a large part in the economy of Castleton since Tudor times; this early scene of Castle Street shows horses and carts waiting outside the George Hotel to take tourists to the station or the caverns. The Bull Hotel is seen in the centre of the photograph, the Castle Hotel to the left. Like today, there are no footpaths to be seen on this street.

The George Hotel, 1948 and 2011

Here we see Castleton residents marching past the George Hotel to the War Memorial in the Market Place in 1948. This hotel was possibly established as an ale house before 1577. The landlord was evicted in 1884 because his family had contracted typhoid fever. In 1891 conveyances ran from the George Hotel to neighbouring villages three times a week. Note the number of first aid men escorting the marchers.

Cryer House, Castle Street, 1950s and 2011

Cryer House was named after a vicar of Castleton during Cromwell's Protectorate. A smaller house, Billson House, had stood on this site before it was purchased in 1658. The Ashton family bought the building in 1702, and it later became part of the Losehill Hall estate until it was sold in 1925. The house has not altered much since the 1700s. The 2011 photograph shows a conservatory which was used a tea room for many years.

The Entrance to Castle Street, 1910 and 2011

Castle Street at this point joins the main highway of the village, called Cross Street. This scene shows people waiting for the arrival of the Castleton Garland King and Queen in 1910. On the left of the scene is the Castle Hotel. On the right in 1809 was Needham's Museum and Petrifaction Shop. Although the shop use has changed, little else has changed since the earlier photograph was taken.

The Castle Hotel, Early 1900s and 2011

The landlord of this inn was fined 11s for brewing beer without a licence in the reign of Charles II. This building has been used as a beer house, court house, post office and mortuary. In 1740 the stagecoach 'John Mills' stopped here on its way to Tideswell. By 1829 the Sheffield to Manchester stagecoach, 'The Wellington', also stopped here daily. The photograph shows the landlord Mr Unsworth and his family..

Castleton Church and Church Yard, 1809 and 2011

Castleton church was originally called the Church of Peak Castle and was built about 1100 as a garrison church to serve the Castle. In the fourteenth century the church was dedicated to the Christian King Edmund. This 1809 view shows the south chancel door and early English thirteenth-century windows. Two gentlemen are walking on the public footpath, which was removed by Act of Parliament in 1861. The windows have been replaced and the south door removed.

Castleton Church, 1880 and 2011

This photograph was taken after the repairs and alterations to the exterior of the church were made between 1820 and 1840. By 2011 the interior has also been remodelled, but the beautiful seventeenth-century pews have been retained, as has the Norman archway. The roof is eighteenth-century. The floor of the nave is made up of headstones where the more important people of the village would have been buried, as there is no crypt.

The Bull's Head Hotel, Cross Street, 1930s and 2011
We are now in Cross Street, so named because a medieval cross once stood on this spot. The Hotel is an old establishment where Daniel Defoe stayed on his visit to Castleton in 1726. Schoolchildren waiting to return to Hope Station are posing for the camera. By the time the 2011 photograph was taken, the windows have been removed and replaced with larger ones and the entrance porch has been removed.

The Nag's Head Hotel, Cross Street, 1920 and 2011
This is another view of the Nag's Head Pub, with young girls from the village and the local band taking part in the Garland Ceremony. Many people are watching from the hotel's windows. The west section, which was originally the coach house, has been demolished to widen the entrance into Back Street. By 2011 the exterior coating to the walls has also been removed to reveal the limestone walling.

The Cruck Barn, Cross Street, 1928 and 2011

The Garland King and Queen are seen passing the old Cruck Barn; built before 1530, it has served as a barn for hundreds of years. Pashley's Blue John Shop's sign is clearly seen. From its building in the fourteenth century until the mid-1900s, a right of way, the coffin route from Edale, passed through this building to the churchyard.

PASHLEY'S

Post Office and Stores,

CROSS ST., CASTLETON

KODAK ... ENSIGN FILMS ...

LOCAL VIEWS AND MAPS. LARGEST AND BEST SELECTION IN THE DISTRICT.

SPECIALITIES:

Blue John and Derbyshire Spar Goods

OF ALL DESCRIPTIONS

Large and small specimens including Vases, Cups, Brooches, Tie Pins, Cuff Links, Rings, Ash Trays, Chalices, etc.

Pashley's Post Office and Stores, Early 1900s and 2011

This scene shows Mr Pashley, his wife and child outside what was the local post office for many years. The Castle Inn or Hotel had served as the post office in the nineteenth century. The building today is a Blue John gift shop. To the right of the building can be seen the north entrance to the churchyard.

Cross Street Looking West, 1905 and 2011

In the centre of this scene can be seen the modern houses that replaced the turnpike road Toll Bar Cottage, demolished in 1886. The building on the extreme right is now the Blue John Craft shop. On the left of the 1905 scene the building with the overhanging awning is the church Toll Bar Cottage, named because before 1634 people from Edale who wished to bury their dead had to pay a toll to enter.

Cross Street Looking East, 1905 and 2011
On the left of the scene can be seen the front of what is now Rose Cottage Tea Rooms. In the centre of this view can be seen two carriages stopped outside the Nag's Head Public House; a motor car travelling west is passing these carriages. At the end of the right-hand row of cottages, a lady in dark clothes is leaving the north entrance to the churchyard and Toll Bar Cottage.

Council Depot, 1955 and 2011

This building has served as a blacksmith's forge, council depot, shop, factory, and now the Peak Park Information Centre and Castleton Historical Society Museum. The main village car park is also on this site. The leet to the medieval water-driven corn mill runs through the car park.

New Hall Bridge, 1890 and 2011
This poor photograph is of New Hall Bridge, erected when the turnpike road was built in 1758, repaired in 1791 after it had suffered damage. On the left is now the Information Centre and Museum. On the right can just be seen the Castleton Restaurant, now the local garage. The house which is at the back of the present garage has not yet been built.

Castleton Women's Unionist Association

A VICTORY

WHIST DRIVE

will be held in the

Castleton Restaurant

ON TUESDAY, NOVEMBER 10th

To Commence at 7.45 p.m.

Admission - 1/- each

8 GOOD PRIZES

Refreshments at popular prices

Castleton Restaurant, Buxton Road, 1920 and 2011

This building was the venue for most of Castleton's entertainments at the beginning of the twentieth century. Dress Balls were held on New Year's Day and Shrove Tuesdays, all lit by gas. The village's first moving picture was shown in the building, with musical accompaniment by a local resident, Mr Barber. The local garage now occupies the site.
Inset: Poster for a whist drive at the Castleton Restaurant, 1918.

Speedwell House, District Headquarters Oldham & District Cyclists' Union, 1920 and 2011
Cycling was a very popular pastime in the early part of the last century. Speedwell House, the headquarters of the Oldham & District Cyclists' Union, provided accommodation with or without board. The building now serves as an outdoor shop. Many villagers provided tea and meals for cyclists and also looked after their cycles for two pennies when they walked on the hills and moors.

Speedwell Café, Buxton Road, 1920 and 2011

In the grounds of Speedwell House was Joseph Eyre's café, which provided tea and meals for visitors and cyclists. In this 1920 scene a group of motorcyclists look as if they have been well provided for. In the 2011 photograph can be seen the building which replaced Eyre's café, Orchard House, built in the late 1980s.

New Hall, Buxton Road, 1860s and 2011

Built in the fifteenth century and remodelled in the late sixteenth and seventeenth centuries, it was the home of an old Castleton family, the Savages, who lost their estates during the Civil War. Another Castleton family the Barbers, later owned the Hall. By 1889 it was in poor repair and had been divided up into a number of labourer's cottages. It was sold in 1890 to make way for the present Methodist church.

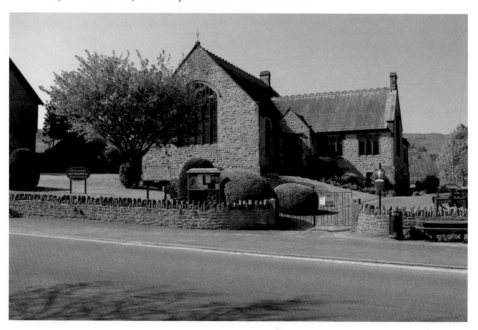

Goosehill Hall, Buxton Road, 1918 and 2011

This photograph is of Goosehill Hall; built before 1670s, it is thought that it has origins in the fourteenth century. The present entrance is off the Buxton Road. The original entrance was at the top of Goosehill. The house was the home of Richard Bagshaw, who was High Sheriff of Derbyshire in 1721. The Hall is haunted by a lady in gray, a phantom horse and a ghostly medieval tournament held in the grounds.

Goosehill, 1970s and 2011

Goosehill is on the original ancient hollow way to the Norman castle. The cottages in this scene were built just after 1621 as two barns and two cottages. The barns have now been converted into cottages and the pebble dashing has been removed from the walls. The old miner's cottage is being rebuilt. A beautiful sycamore tree in the centre of the scene has been removed.

Goosehill, 1920s and 2011
This 1920s scene shows the back of a group of buildings built in the 1620s. The miner's cottage in the centre has been demolished and replaced by a modern house. The building to the extreme right was originally two barns and has now been converted to housing. Many of the cottages have been adapted and enlarged since this picture was taken.

**Goosehill Bridge,
1770 and 2011**
The original Goosehill
Bridge replaced some
stepping stones
(Slippery Stones)
which crossed the river
at this point. The area
is named after the de
Grousel family, who
owned land in this
part of Castleton in
the fifteenth century.
In 1770 the bridge
had three spans, as
the river was much
wider and flooded. The
present bridge was
built when the river
bed was deepened
to take flood waters.
Apart from this
channelling, there has
been very little change
in this part of the
village for hundreds of
years.

The Waterside and Goosehill Bridge, 1905 and 2011

This is a view of Goosehill Bridge and the Waterside in 1915. The building on the right is Dolly's Grocery Shop. The tall building to the centre in both photographs was increased in height after 1871 and used as a museum by John Tym until 1885. The low, small building to the left of John Tym's building has served as a bicycle repair shop.

The Waterside, 1908 and 2011

Just beyond the house on the left is Russet Well, used by villagers for hundreds of years as a water source until piped water was installed. The pathway on the right leads to Peak Cavern. In the centre of this scene a doorway leads to a cottage, Rose Cottage, now demolished. The bricked-up entrance can still be seen. Soldiers from the nearby army summer camp are enjoying the view.

Goosehill Green, 1920s and 2011

This is a photograph of Goosehill, taken in the 1920s, showing Mrs. Payne's Tea Garden. The miners' cottage on the right has disappeared and was replaced in the 1980s. The barn to the left of the row of cottages, built in 1622, has also been converted into residential property. Mrs Payne's property, then two cottages, is now one cottage.

Peak Cavern Walk, 1890 and 2011

Peak Cavern Walk in 1890 gives an indication of how irregular cottage building was in past centuries in Castleton. The building with the three windows in the centre of the view, Rose Cottage, was demolished in the late nineteenth century and became Mrs Payne's tea garden. The building with the arched window was the site of the school between 1835 and 1851.

Peak Cavern Walk, Slack's Mineral Shop, 1900 and 2011 This building was the Peak Cavern public house in 1794 and continued as such until after 1830. This photograph shows it as Slack's mineral shop, which sold curios and Blue John at the beginning of the twentieth century. Today it is a holiday cottage.

The Candle Factory, Hollowford Lane, Castleton

In the nineteenth century candles were made in this building. They were used by the local villagers, and also by the lead miners as their only method of lighting in the dark and dangerous mines. The vats used to boil the tallow to make the candles can now be seen at the front of the Methodist church on Buxton Road. The wicks for the candles were made by the rope makers at Peak Cavern.

Peak Cavern Entrance, 1890 and 1950

Peak Cavern is a large cave, first shown on a map in 1250, used by local rope makers until well into the twentieth century. In the seventeenth century it was the home of 'Cock Lorrell', the last king of the beggars. Ben Jonson called him the 'the most notorious knave that ever lived'. The small one-storey cottage on the bottom right in the earlier view was last occupied in the late nineteenth century.

Peak Cavern Walk, 1910 and 2011
This is the very old walkway to Peak Cavern first mentioned by the Anglo-Norman Henry of Huntington. The Walk had been used by prehistoric man and, later, the Saxons before the Normans came. Others to have used this track were Henry II in 1157, Edward I in 1290, Daniel Defoe in 1726, Queen Victoria in 1842 and Lord Byron as a fourteen-year-old.

Peak Cavern Entrance, Looking Out, 1810 and 2011
The rope makers began to use the cavern mouth in about the mid-eighteenth century. The ropes and twine were used by the local lead mining industry. Here we see three Edwardian ladies looking at the rope walk where the fibres were stretched and twisted to make the ropes. Today, the rope-making instruments are still there, but the houses once used by the rope makers' families have been demolished. The last person to live in the cavern was Mary Knight, over 150 years ago.
Inset: Poster, Peak Cavern, early twentieth century.

Lunnon's Back, Goosehill, 1930 and 2011
Lunnon's Back is an old trackway to Peak Cavern from Goosehill. The cottage to the right of both these views was one of the very early brew houses in the village. The building on the left was a barn in 1930 but has since been converted to housing.

Lead Miner's Cottage, Goosehill, 1900
Many of the cottages in Castleton were
originally two-roomed lead miners'
cottages. This photograph shows one
of the last of the lead miners' cottages
in Castleton. At one time a family of
eight children lived in this two-roomed
building. It has now been rebuilt and
enlarged. The picture below is of Joseph
Hall, an old lead miner of Castleton.

Bridge Cottage, Goosehill Bridge, Early 1900s and 2011
The Castleton Garland King rides the boundaries of the village every Garland day before the start of the ceremony. Here he is shown outside Bridge Cottage, built in the seventeenth century. Originally two cottages, it is now one residence. The large house shown replaced the lead miner's cottage referred to in the photograph on the previous page.

Stones Bottom, Goosehill Bridge, 1930 and 2011

Stones Bottom is an old trackway which in early medieval times led over the river, up Goosehill and then on to the entrance to Peveril Castle. The building on the right is now Carlton Emporium. The third floor, built to house a museum in the nineteenth century, can be seen. The building on the extreme right was a two-roomed cottage and is now a glass and jewellery shop.

Dolly's Café, Stones Bottom, Goosehill Bridge, 1926 and 2011
This shop was owned by a resident of Castleton who died aged over 100 years old. Here she is seen standing outside her shop with her husband in 1930. Australian fruit and apples were sold, as can be seen in the window. The building is still called Dolly's Café today.

John Tym's Shop and Museum, Stones Bottom, 1871 and 2011
John Tym's shop and museum has been enlarged with a third floor. Stockport Town Council appointed John Tym curator of its museum in 1885 when he was declared bankrupt. The building now houses the Carlton Emporium. The 2011 photograph shows the present owner standing in the doorway.

Treacle Street, Stones Bottom, 1910 and 2011
Treacle Street was a narrow laneway leading off Stones Bottom. The buildings on the right comprised at least three cottages. It is rumoured to have been Castleton's red light district at some time in the past. All the properties are now incorporated into one residence.

The Douglas Museum, 1924 and 2011

The Douglas Museum, which lasted from 1920 to 1978, called 'The House of Wonders,' was often visited by Houdini, a great friend of Douglas. Randolph Douglas was a skilled miniaturist and model maker who also exhibited carvings and models from all over the world. A number of the exhibits can now be seen in the Castleton Historical Society Museum in the Visitor Centre. The Museum name board can be seen on the wall in the 1924 photograph.

Inset: Poster for the Douglas Museum, twentieth century.

Slippery Stones or Sodom, 1930 and 2011
This photograph entitled Sodom shows Slippery Stones in 1930. Why this view should be called Sodom is a mystery. On the right is another view of the Douglas Museum. The large trees on the left of the road have gone and a new building development is in progress in 2011.

The Turnpike Road and Toll Bar (Buxton Road), 1800 and 2011
The Sheffield to Sparrowpit Turnpike Road, built in 1758, wound its way up Winnats Pass. A new turnpike road was opened in 1802 to bypass this difficult climb. This old print shows the stagecoach leaving Castleton on its way to Manchester. On the left can be seen the toll house and gate, which was demolished in July 1886. The road is now the main road to Buxton and Manchester.

The YMCA Volunteer Tents, Castleton Camp, the Flattes, 1904 and 2011
These fields were granted by King Henry VII in 1486 to Thomas Savage, whose family built the New Hall on the land in the 1500s. The land was used for a number of years at the beginning of the twentieth century by army volunteer units on exercises. This photograph shows the YMCA Volunteer Tents on the site in 1904. The land is now pasture for cattle and sheep.

Speedwell Mine, 1890 and 1910
Speedwell Mine, at the foot of Winnats Pass, was hacked through the rock by miners in search of lead in the 1770s. The mine closed after two decades due to the limited amount of lead it produced. It is now a show mine, visited by thousands of tourists every year. These Edwardian visitors are waiting to enter the mine. The Pass is now the only roadway out of the village to the west.

Speedwell Mine, Late 1800s and 2011

The early view is another illustration of Speedwell Mine. In the mid-1750s, the building on the left was a 'beer house' called the Navigation Inn. It was called Speedwell because drinkers gave the salutation 'speed-well' to those adventurous travellers about to attempt Winnats Pass. It was still a 'beer house' in 1809. By 1829, the mine was an established tourist attraction. Sheep still roam the road and hillside today.

Speedwell Mine, 1945 and 2011
This view shows the lonely and rugged country above Speedwell Mine. Even in 1945 it was a desolate place. It is reputedly about this spot that a young couple were murdered in the mid-eighteenth century. The demand by tourists led to the opening of a larger car park, shown in the 2011 view.

Winnats Pass, 1910 and 2011

The name Winnats Pass is derived from 'Wind Gates' and it is an impressive High Peak limestone gorge about one mile in length. This view shows a lone carriage going down the pass about 1910. The new 1819 turnpike bypassed this road, which led to its disuse. A single electrical cable can be seen bringing electricity to farms high on the moors.

Winnats Pass, 1930s and 2011

This is a later view of the old Saltway from Cheshire to Sheffield. The trackway is still an unmade road but there has been an increase in the demand for electricity, as can be seen by the number of electricity cables on the poles, which were later all placed underground. This remote spot is reputed to be where a couple, Allan and Clara, were murdered in 1758 by Castleton men. The saddle reputedly used by Clara is pictured. The saddle can still be seen in Speedwell Mine.

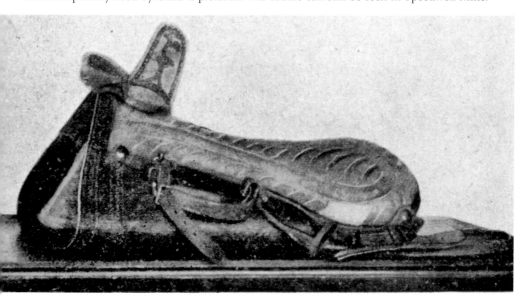

Toll Pike Road, 1910 and 2011

The main turnpike road to Manchester was built in 1819 to bypass the route through Winnats Pass. The road was built on shale, which was continually eroded by rain, frost and heavy traffic. The road finally collapsed in the 1950s and, after a number of attempts to repair it, was closed. The 2011 photograph shows the collapsed section of the road, which is still today sliding down the hill side.

Odin Mine, 1800s and 2011

Odin Mine, thought to have been mined by the Romans for lead, is referred to in documents of 1280. This mine's heyday for production was from 1704 to 1867. The industry had almost died out by the late 1800s in the Castleton area. Many miners were killed working the mines, and many were killed in Castleton mines.

Treak Cliff Cavern, 1950s and 2011

Treak Cliff Cavern is a geologically important Site of Special Scientific Interest. Blue John stone deposits are regularly mined here. It opened as a show cave in 1945. This view shows the entrance to the mine in the 1950s. The 2011 photograph shows the pathway up to the mine from the old turnpike road. The name Treak Cliff is derived from the fact that a 'Hanging Tree' once stood on this cliff side.

Pindale Road, 1905 and 2011

This scene looks east over an old part of the village which was just outside of the medieval ditch enclosure. There have been few changes to the exterior of the cottages – the pebble dash and the low walls have been removed. A number of these buildings are now holiday cottages.

Acknowledgements

The compilation of a book like this can only be accomplished with the goodwill and assistance of many people. Without my wife Jane, none of the books or projects I have undertaken in recent years would have been possible. Much of the information in this book has flowered as a result of discussions and conversation with local people over many years. Thanks to all of them.

All of the modern and the majority of old photographs are from the author's own collection, acquired over a number of years. I would like to thank Castleton Historical Society Trustees for permission to use the old images on pages 11, 13, 19, 20, 22, 28, 45, 48, 51, 61, 78 and 80. I would also wish to thank Mrs J. Hall for permission to reproduce the drawing on page 77 and Mrs J. Adamson for permission to use the photograph on page 42.